I0453997

REFLECTIONS
AND PRAYERS ### ON
Sacred Romance

ELIZABETH GRIEST

Inks and Bindings
888-290-5218
www.inksandbindings.com
orders@inksandbindings.com

Contents

Dear Reader:

I Believe Sacred Romance between Women and Men is Deeply Wanted/Needed by some individuals.

May such souls be blessed by my thoughts/feelings and prayers on Holy Romance.

Space is provided for readers own reflections and/or prayers.

Prayers/Blessings
Elizabeth Griest

I

I've been through so much Suffering with partners.

I speak for many individuals here.

Sacred Mother God/Sacred Father God show us what to do to Receive the Sacred partners You have for each of us.

_____

_____

_____

_____

_____

_____

_____

_____

_____

_____

_____

_____

_____

_____

_____

_____

_____

_____

_____

II

Sacred Parents of All, my words can apply to many souls.

Divine Parents of All, You and I know I'm Highly Sensitive and thus can be easily hurt.

We further know I am prone to resentment caused by soul wounds.

Such resentment fuels deep guilt and a strong sense of being unworthy to receive my Sacred partner.

Heal me of such pain. Show me how to cooperate with You in my Healing, Sacred Parents of All.

_____

_____

_____

_____

_____

_____

_____

_____

_____

_____

_____

III

My Right/Resonant man is a Celestial Combination
of Care Giver and Romantic partner.

_____

_____

_____

_____

_____

_____

_____

_____

_____

_____

_____

_____

_____

_____

_____

_____

_____

_____

_____

_____

_____

_____

IV

I will be my Sacred partner's Caregiver and Romantic partner.

_____

_____

_____

_____

_____

_____

_____

_____

_____

_____

_____

_____

_____

_____

_____

_____

_____

_____

_____

_____

_____

_____

_____

V

Truly, I Believe Sacred Mother God Needs to be Recognized/Revered Equally as much as Sacred Father God does for Women and Men to be Sacred partners.

VI

⊹·❖·⊹

Sacred Parents of All Desire Sacred partners to
be United to do Good for themselves and others.

VII

Actually, I Believe United Sacred partners can do so much more Good than Unjoined Sacred partners.

_____

_____

_____

_____

_____

_____

_____

_____

_____

_____

_____

_____

_____

_____

_____

_____

_____

_____

_____

_____

_____

_____

VIII

Sacred partners share a Joint Holy Purpose –
something they are to do together. Something that
melds their individual talents/skills in ways that
Honor Divine Parents of All/that Benefits Divine
partners that Benefits others.

_____

_____

_____

_____

_____

_____

_____

_____

_____

_____

_____

_____

_____

_____

_____

_____

_____

_____

_____

_____

_____

IX

To me, Sacred Romance means Sacred Partners not only possess a Shared Divine Destiny; but also a Fundamentally Deep Appreciation of each other.

_____

_____

_____

_____

_____

_____

_____

_____

_____

_____

_____

_____

_____

_____

_____

_____

_____

_____

_____

X

Sacred partners' Deep Appreciation of each other is rooted in Sacred Trust consisting of Gentle Honesty and Genuine Reliability between Sacred partners.

_____

_____

_____

_____

_____

_____

_____

_____

_____

_____

_____

_____

_____

_____

_____

_____

_____

_____

_____

_____

XI

Sacred partners are able to resolve their differences via Deep Trust/Genuine Empathy/Genuine Kindness/Prayer to Sacred Parents of All.

_____

_____

_____

_____

_____

_____

_____

_____

_____

_____

_____

_____

_____

_____

_____

_____

_____

_____

_____

_____

XII

Prayers by Sacred partners which lead to, and/or necessitate Wise/Merciful actions are often the Most Powerfully Answered Prayers.

_____

_____

_____

_____

_____

_____

_____

_____

_____

_____

_____

_____

_____

_____

_____

_____

_____

_____

_____

XIII

Just as Prayers to Sacred Parents of All can draw
Sacred partners, so can Prayers to Divine Parents
of All help resolve Sacred partners' differences.

_____

_____

_____

_____

_____

_____

_____

_____

_____

_____

_____

_____

_____

_____

_____

_____

_____

_____

_____

_____

_____

_____

XIV

One's Sacred Destiny means Living/Doing what one Loves which Benefits oneself and others.

_____

_____

_____

_____

_____

_____

_____

_____

_____

_____

_____

_____

_____

_____

_____

_____

_____

_____

_____

_____

_____

_____

_____

XV

Divine Destinies are partly Universal plus partly Individualized.

Universal in that I Believe everyone is meant to grow in Empathy/Kindness/Prayer for oneself and others – including animals, plants, the Earth as well as for people.

Individualized in that I Believe each Soul has a Special Unique Role to Play via one's own Talents/ Skills/Heart's Desire/Experiences.

_____

_____

_____

_____

_____

_____

_____

_____

_____

_____

_____

_____

_____

_____

XVI

Sacred Parents of All, I Believe Everybody Has an Inner Child.

Further, I Believe everyone's Inner Child holds one's Deepest Feelings and Beliefs about oneself/others/God/Life.

The Inner Child keeps one's Memories of this and Past Lives – so, I Believe.

Too, the Inner Child carries the Blueprint for one's Divine Destiny.

The Inner Child Needs one's Adult Self as well as Divine Parents of All to truly Realize/Live one's Divine Destiny.

_____

_____

_____

_____

_____

_____

_____

_____

_____

_____

XVII

Divine Parents of All, My Inner Child and I Need the Removal of All Blockages to Receiving my Sacred Partner.

Chief among these Blockages is resentment and its resulting feeling of unworthiness to have my Divine partner.

Also, my Child Self and I harbor some false beliefs that the only man I deserve is a cruel/selfish one; plus, most men are cruel/selfish.

Heal me of these Blockages/Beliefs.

Guide/Guard me in exactly what I'm to do to help my Healing.

_____

_____

_____

_____

_____

_____

_____

_____

_____

XVIII

The Inner Child is Crucial in Divine Romance; for, the Child Self can Intuitively/Instinctively Sense who's the Right/Resonant partner.

However, it's Imperative the Inner Child be Absolutely Honest about Deep Needs and Wants. And, not become impaled by what the Child Self feels should Need/Want based upon unhealed soul pain, others' expectations, etc.

XIX

The Female Inner Child Intuitively senses Soul Resonance if she allows herself to.

The Male Inner Child can Intuitively sense Soul Resonance; but, can be more likely to be distracted by his sex drive, plus the female's appearance.

_____

_____

_____

_____

_____

_____

_____

_____

_____

_____

_____

_____

_____

_____

_____

_____

_____

_____

XX

However crucial the Inner Child is in determining one's Sacred partner; still it's Absolutely Essential for the Child Self to be Guided/Guarded by the Adult Self; and, of course, Sacred Parents of All.

_____

_____

_____

_____

_____

_____

_____

_____

_____

_____

_____

_____

_____

_____

_____

_____

_____

_____

_____

_____

XXI

Universal - as in Shared-Human Wants/Needs/ Traits exist in Women and Men They are Wanting and Needing to Receive and Give True Love, as well as Desiring to Attract and Seek True Love.

_____

_____

_____

_____

_____

_____

_____

_____

_____

_____

_____

_____

_____

_____

_____

_____

_____

_____

_____

XXII

It seems to me Females possess Universal as well as Individual Needs/Wants/Traits. Universal plus Individual Needs/Wants/Traits applies to Males also.

_____

_____

_____

_____

_____

_____

_____

_____

_____

_____

_____

_____

_____

_____

_____

_____

_____

_____

_____

_____

_____

XXIII

It appears to me Female Universally are Receivers/Givers in their Wants/Needs/Traits in Sacred Romance.

_____

_____

_____

_____

_____

_____

_____

_____

_____

_____

_____

_____

_____

_____

_____

_____

_____

_____

_____

_____

XXIV

I see Male Universally as Givers/Receivers in their
Wants/Needs/Traits in Sacred Romance.

XXV

In my view, it's incumbent upon sacred partners to learn their partner's Unique Wants/Needs/Traits.

_____

_____

_____

_____

_____

_____

_____

_____

_____

_____

_____

_____

_____

_____

_____

_____

_____

_____

_____

_____

_____

_____

XXVI

I Believe it's essential for Sacred partners to Honor and Attend to their partner's Unique Wants/ Needs/Traits.

_____

_____

_____

_____

_____

_____

_____

_____

_____

_____

_____

_____

_____

_____

_____

_____

_____

_____

_____

_____

_____

XXVII

It is Well to Frequently Recall Sacred Romance is Rooted in Right/Resonant Communication/Companionship.

Because Sacred partners are human relational Imbalances can occur.

Sacred partners are imperfect beings; yet mystically under Sacred Parents of All's Guidance/Guardianship Sacred partners are Perfect for each other.

_____

_____

_____

_____

_____

_____

_____

_____

_____

_____

_____

_____

_____

XXVIII

It is Wise to remember to Remedy/Rectify Imbalances between Sacred partners.

I Believe the Best Way to do so is seeking Sacred Guidance/Guardianship from Sacred Parents of All.

Our Divine Parents of All Work Directly with individual partners as well as Indirectly with others assisting Sacred Heart partners.

_____

_____

_____

_____

_____

_____

_____

_____

_____

_____

_____

_____

_____

_____

_____

_____

_____

_____

XXIX

Once Sacred partners meet/sense they have truly found each other it is crucial for them to Pray for Divine Protection from Divine Parents of All.

_____

_____

_____

_____

_____

_____

_____

_____

_____

_____

_____

_____

_____

_____

_____

_____

_____

_____

_____

_____

XXX

Sacred Protection from Sacred Parents of All is Necessary against human and evil entities interference.

_____

_____

_____

_____

_____

_____

_____

_____

_____

_____

_____

_____

_____

_____

_____

_____

_____

_____

_____

_____

_____

XXXI

How I wish it weren't so! But, there are demons plus evil entities. The latter being some departed humans still gripped by evil influences; also, evil beings who never were human.

Thus, it is Wise to recall to seek Our Sacred Parents of All's Protection.

Sacred partnerships especially require Divine Protection because the evil of all sources wants to destroy the Sacred Union of Sacred partnerships.

Further, this particularly applies to the Inner Child of each other Sacred partner; for, the Child Self is the human root of Sacred partnerships.

_____

_____

_____

_____

_____

_____

_____

_____

_____

_____

_____

XXXII

I Believe Women and Men were created to Help
Balance, Fulfill, and Complement each other.

_____

_____

_____

_____

_____

_____

_____

_____

_____

_____

_____

_____

_____

_____

_____

_____

_____

_____

_____

_____

_____

XXXIII

Genuine Holy Romance is Beautiful Beyond Words,
so I Believe.

XXXIV

I Believe Holy Romance is a Mystical Blend of the Universal with the Individualized.

XXXV

Living Holy Romance with one's Sacred partner
Greatly Aids each partner in Living the Holy Life.

_____

_____

_____

_____

_____

_____

_____

_____

_____

_____

_____

_____

_____

_____

_____

_____

_____

_____

_____

_____

_____

XXXVI

Sacred Romance when lived by each partner can
Mean Far Greater Health; Physical/Emotional/
Mental/Spiritual for both partners.

So, I Intuit.

_____

_____

_____

_____

_____

_____

_____

_____

_____

_____

_____

_____

_____

_____

_____

_____

_____

_____

_____

_____

XXXVII

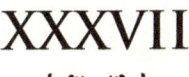

If a girl grows up feeling treated as second-best she as a woman will often attract men who treat her as second-best to someone or something else.

XXXVIII

A girl/woman must know/feel/emanate she is worthy of first-class regard/treatment.

XXXIX

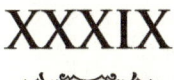

A girl/woman Taking Care for her health and appearance is telling herself and others she Deserves Good Treatment.

_____

_____

_____

_____

_____

_____

_____

_____

_____

_____

_____

_____

_____

_____

_____

_____

_____

_____

_____

_____

_____

XXXX

Much of a girl's/woman's Good self-treatment consists of following Soul Felt wants rather than others' imposed shoulds.

XXXXI

Some shoulds are necessary, even beneficial; but, many are enslaving.

Following such ones mostly stems from fear of disapproval and/or abandonment.

_____

_____

_____

_____

_____

_____

_____

_____

_____

_____

_____

_____

_____

_____

_____

_____

_____

_____

_____

XXXXII

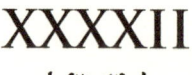

I Believe a part of a woman's Inner Child wants a male partner, who like a Kind father, treats her well.

Just as I Believe a part of a man's Inner Child wants a female partner, who like a Kind mother, treats him well.

_____

_____

_____

_____

_____

_____

_____

_____

_____

_____

_____

_____

_____

_____

_____

_____

_____

_____

XXXXIII

I think it helps men to value women by men being in touch with their Inner Child need for a mother, yet, not remaining at a Childish level.

_____
_____
_____
_____
_____
_____
_____
_____
_____
_____
_____
_____
_____
_____
_____
_____
_____
_____
_____
_____
_____

XXXXIV

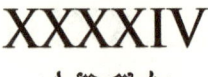

It seems to me it's well for a man to give proactively, initiatively to a woman he genuinely cares about.

Thus acting upon his adult need for a female partner as well as his Inner Boy's need for mother.

_____

_____

_____

_____

_____

_____

_____

_____

_____

_____

_____

_____

_____

_____

_____

_____

_____

_____

XXXXV

It often appears many men desire sex first, companionship second.

Further, it helps many men to practice some sacrificial giving by honoring many women's need for companionship first, and sex second.

_____

_____

_____

_____

_____

_____

_____

_____

_____

_____

_____

_____

_____

_____

_____

_____

_____

_____

_____

_____

XXXXVI

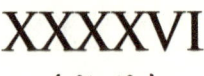

A man needs to know what makes his woman happy
so that he can be made happy in return.

_____
_____
_____
_____
_____
_____
_____
_____
_____
_____
_____
_____
_____
_____
_____
_____
_____
_____
_____
_____
_____
_____

XXXXVII

Spiritual Aristocracy is a Vital Component of
Sacred Romance – the Soul to Soul Union of
Female and Male.

So, I Believe.

XXXXVIII

Spiritual Aristocracy/Spiritual Nobility is Not necessarily lineage nor formal education nor money; but, rather, an Innate Courtesy and Caring for self and others. Others are all people as well as animals, plants, the Earth.

_____
_____
_____
_____
_____
_____
_____
_____
_____
_____
_____
_____
_____
_____
_____
_____
_____
_____
_____
_____

XXXXIX

Spiritual Aristocracy is Fairness, Honesty in Word and Deed. It is a Genuine Efforts to Speak the Truth via Loving Kindness and Empathy. Spiritual Nobility also means living one's Divine Destiny.

XXXXX

I earnestly pray for all souls who desire Sacred Romance to quickly/easily know it/live it.

XXXXXI

Sacred Parents of All, for all Your children who long for Sacred Romance, Grant it to them via Your Unfathomable Grace and Mercy.

_____

_____

_____

_____

_____

_____

_____

_____

_____

_____

_____

_____

_____

_____

_____

_____

_____

_____

_____

_____

_____

_____

XXXXXII

Divine Parents of All, help all Your children live as
Spiritual Aristocrats whether or not they choose
Sacred Romance.

Thank You, Sacred Parents of All.

_____
_____
_____
_____
_____
_____
_____
_____
_____
_____
_____
_____
_____
_____
_____
_____
_____
_____
_____
_____

www.ingramcontent.com/pod-product-compliance
Lightning Source LLC
Chambersburg PA
CBHW020342130626
46549CB00003B/1253